Uncle Ben's Fishing Trip

By Gretchen Brassington

Illustrated by David Preston Smith

🔟 Dominie Press, Inc.

Publisher: Raymond Yuen
Project Editor: John S. F. Graham
Editor: Bob Rowland
Designer: Greg DiGenti
Illustrator: David Preston Smith

Published by:

ᴚ Dominie Press, Inc.

1949 Kellogg Avenue
Carlsbad, California 92008 USA

www.dominie.com

1-800-232-4570

Paperback ISBN 0-7685-0427-9
Printed in Singapore by PH Productions Pte Ltd
1 2 3 4 5 6 PH 05 04 03

Table of Contents

Chapter One
Fishing on
the Wild Waves

The *Sea Flight* rose up to meet each wave, broke through the crest, and then fell back down onto the sea. Kevin grew dizzy watching the constant rush and surge of water, and the bucking-horse motion was making him feel decidedly green.

He leaned forward at the boat rail and rested his head on his folded arms. He couldn't—just couldn't—be seasick in front of his uncle and cousin Cassie!

Kevin sighed. Cassie had changed. In the old days they used to live along the same country road. They would spend all of their free time playing together, spending hours and hours under the cottonwood trees down by the creek. They got filthy searching for snakes under stones and chasing rabbits in the long grass with Cassie's dog, Rowdy.

Then Uncle Ben and Aunt Judy moved away to Hawaii, and cousin Cassie went with them. Kevin really missed her.

Now, two years later, they were back. They moved into a new home in another town. It was farther away than before, but Kevin didn't mind. He took the bus

to stay over for a weekend.

The house was near the ocean. It was strange seeing those same people in a different place. Uncle Ben and Aunt Judy were pretty much the same. But Cassie was different. She was quiet and distant, hardly saying a word.

To be fair, Kevin knew he hadn't talked much, either, but that was because he didn't know what to say to her anymore. Cassie was like a stranger.

There was something else, too. It hadn't occurred to Kevin earlier, but because his aunt and uncle's new home wasn't far from the ocean, they would be spending a lot of time in the water.

"I know all boys like boats," Uncle Ben had said. "So I rented one for the whole weekend." With his big arms around Kevin's shoulders, he drew him close.

"To tell the truth, I'm really looking forward to some fishing."

"Just don't ask me to go with you," Kevin's aunt had laughed. "You won't get me anywhere near water!"

Kevin wished he had spoken up right then, and told them that he had always hated the ocean. He hated how deep it was and all the creepy things in it. He hated getting dumped on by waves and spitting sand out of his mouth. He hated everything about it.

But the moment was gone, and now he couldn't disappoint his uncle.

So there they were, out on a fishing trip on a sunny day, doing exactly what Kevin hated to do. And Cassie was still unfriendly. Maybe she saw how terrible he was on a boat and thought he was a weakling.

Kevin knew that if his uncle asked him to fish, he really would be sick. And Cassie would know then, for sure, what a wimp he was.

Chapter Two
Whale! Starboard!

"How about setting up some trolling lures for me, Kevin," Uncle Ben called from the cabin.

Kevin turned his head. "What?"

"The lures. They're in the fish box there. Just hook them up to the lines and

rods." To Kevin, Uncle Ben was speaking another language.

Kevin crouched over the open box of assorted nylon coils and swivels and bright, plastic, fish-shaped lures with big steel hooks on their bellies. The stench of old fish set him back on his heels.

Uncle Ben slowed the engine until the boat was barely moving in the water. They were sliding slowly up and over the wave tops instead of cutting through them. There was a soft breeze now. The contents of the fish box stained the air like a bad taste in Kevin's mouth, and he closed his eyes on the memory of once before being made sick by that smell. His stomach turned.

Uncle Ben came out onto the deck.

"Dreaming, Kevin? I'll help you set up those lures. You've probably never done this before, have you?" He bent over the fish box.

Kevin saw that Cassie had moved into the helm seat and was piloting the boat. "Will she be all right in there by herself?" Kevin asked. It seemed pretty dangerous for a nine-year-old to be in charge of a boat.

Uncle Ben laughed. "We're not exactly in Grand Central Station, Kevin. There's nothing out here for us to bump into."

Uncle Ben laid several of the nylon coils on the deck and lined up the plastic fish lures. "Which ones do you think will do the job?" he asked.

Fortunately, Uncle Ben chose them

himself, three of the brightest lures with feathered tails and lines of glitter down their sides.

The hooks didn't have to be baited. Kevin was thankful he didn't have to mess with worms or salmon eggs.

Uncle Ben attached the lures and their nylon coils to the fishing reels at the back of the boat. He let out the lines until the lures were trailing through the boat's wake, skipping over the foam like real fish.

Kevin and Uncle Ben sat on the cushioned lockers behind the cabin, in the shade of the flybridge, and watched the lures skittering along behind the boat. This was going to be OK, Kevin thought, as long as they didn't catch anything. He leaned his head against the cabin wall and relaxed.

"Whale! Starboard!" Cassie shouted. She spun the wheel over, and the boat lurched.

Chapter Three
Sailing by
a Stone Dinosaur

"**C**assie! Watch out for the lures!"
Uncle Ben raced back into the cabin.

Cassie pulled back on the wheel and
Kevin's suddenly wide-open eyes saw the
boat's wake carve a crazy S behind them.

Uncle Ben switched off the engine.

Kevin looked around for the whale. He cautiously put his head around the corner of the cabin and sucked in his breath.

The whale lay still and solid in the water. "It's *huge*," Kevin thought. "And it's so quiet."

Something he'd never experienced before reached out and made him unafraid. He stared and stared, hardly breathing.

"Amazing!" he whispered.

In the stillness, Uncle Ben heard him. "It sure is amazing," he said.

Then, perhaps the whale felt the boat had drifted close enough, and it gently began to dive down below the waves, its skin melting into the deep, blue water. There was a soft sigh, and a ghost of vapor *whooshed* into the air.

Then it was gone. Only the puff of vapor remained.

"Wow," Kevin said, breathless.

They continued on, east of a rocky island that lay hunched in the water like a crouching dinosaur. Kevin watched sea birds sunbathing on its high ledges and playing tag over its cliff faces. Maybe the island was alive, like the whale. Maybe it was a dinosaur that had gone to sleep so many centuries ago it had turned to stone.

Could a stone dinosaur wake up? Three radio antennae as bright as needles caught the light of the sun, like three needles growing out of the dinosaur's back. Kevin wondered if the dinosaur knew they were there, or if they had already become part of it.

Kevin saw a lighthouse on the

dinosaur's bony skull as they passed north of the island. It gleamed white, like a single stubby candle. "Happy twenty-first century, dinosaur," Kevin whispered.

Chapter Four

So Much to See in the Sunlit Sea

By midmorning Kevin had forgotten about feeling sick. There was so much to see, even this far out from land.

Something splashed up close, right under Kevin's feet. At that moment, a small, torpedo-shaped fish shot out from the boat's shadow and took flight, scattering a rainbow of diamond droplets from its wide-spread wings.

"Look at the wings on that fish," Kevin murmured. "They must be big fins—if it really *is* a fish."

The creature flew in a long, curving

arch, silvery in the sunlight, and then it was gone in a gliding dive, deep into the side of a wave.

"Did I really see that?" Kevin wondered. He leaned on the boat rail, staring into the water beside the boat, curious to see if there were any more flying fish down there.

The sun shafted deep down into the water, spreading out its light through layers of water, which radiated different tones of blue.

Right at the edge of where the sun could penetrate, Kevin noticed a current stirring, slight and rhythmical, as regular as a heartbeat. He could almost believe that the sea was breathing.

"Beware, for I am all powerful!"

Kevin jumped. Cassie had suddenly appeared beside him.

She hung over the rail, too, staring down. "Don't take risks with me," she chanted softly, leaning farther out over the water. "Don't ever forget I am deep, deep, deep." Before Kevin could say anything she was gone again, her footsteps almost silent on the deck.

"Cassie?" he shouted after her. But she had gone to the front of the boat.

"That's how she used to be," Kevin thought with surprise. "How we both used to be. Imagining things and having adventures!"

Cassie was standing inside the triangle of the bow, leaning her arms on the steel boat rail and looking into the distance. Kevin wondered if he'd imagined what had just happened.

"She's so sure of things now," Kevin thought. "She's confident. She can steer the boat, she wasn't fazed by the whale. But maybe she can feel two ways at once. Maybe she can still pretend, and turn the world into something she imagined."

"Schooling fish!" Cassie shouted, pointing ahead of the boat. Kevin saw a rough patch on the sea that rippled as if the water were boiling. Uncle Ben changed direction, and they circled around the spot, herding the fish so they wouldn't scatter.

"They're just the bait for us," Uncle Ben called from the cabin. "What we want is to hook onto whatever's after them."

Then behind them there was a *Snap-Snap-Snap!* The three lures trailing behind the boat disappeared under the water, and the lines pulled tight. The three reels whirred into action on their rods.

"Kevin!" Cassie shouted. She ran the length of the boat to the back rail. "Take one of the rods. We have to reel them in before they get away."

Kevin reluctantly followed Cassie's lead and took one of the rods out of its holder. He put his hand on the reel handle and immediately felt the strength and urgency of the pull on the other end of the line.

"Slip your hook, fish," he said silently, remembering the silver wings of the flying fish. "Slip your hook and *escape!* I don't want to have to pull you out of the water with everyone watching me."

Chapter Five
Kevin's Big Catch

"Put some muscle into it, Kevin!"
Uncle Ben shouted.

Uncle Ben came out on deck and snatched up the third rod. He immediately began reeling in the line like an expert.

Slowly, Kevin's fingers turned on the

handle of his own reel. He felt the line point down farther. His fish was diving down deeper, and then the line slackened. It had gotten away!

Kevin reeled in the slack line steadily. Then his heart sank. He saw a silver shape come spiraling up through the shadowy water, right where his line was.

"Keep that line tight, Kevin!" Uncle Ben shouted.

Kevin now noticed that Uncle Ben and Cassie were watching him. Had they already reeled in their fish? He didn't know.

Kevin couldn't delay any longer. His fish suddenly came to life and fought on the end of his line.

"It's a beauty!" Cassie said.

Uncle Ben leaned over the rail with a long-handled net and scooped Kevin's fish out of the water. Then he put the fish on the deck and let the net fall around it. The fish stretched its jaws wide and flapped its body inside the net.

Then Uncle Ben took a narrow-bladed knife out of his pocket. Kevin suddenly felt very sick. He shut his eyes tight.

"It's a great-looking fish, Kevin," he heard Cassie say.

Kevin opened his eyes. Uncle Ben and the fish were gone, away to the front of the boat. Had she noticed that he had closed his eyes?

"Dad's fish slipped its hook, and mine was too small," she said. "I threw it back."

"I guess they learned not to chase lures," Kevin said.

He still felt sick. He wondered about that fish that Uncle Ben had taken away.

Cassie came toward him and stood

near the railing. "Remember when we were kids," she said, "and we caught that snake, and Rowdy ate it?"

Kevin nodded. He remembered it vividly. He had been sick to his stomach, but he tried not to let Cassie know.

"I knew that upset you," Cassie said.

"You did?"

"It's only because you love animals," she said. "You're just sensitive."

"I think it's more that I'm squeamish," Kevin said.

"You know, you've only been fishing for a few hours now," she said. "I've been doing it for the last couple of years with Dad. You shouldn't be so hard on yourself for being sensitive. It's a good thing." She grinned. "Tell you what. You don't have to fish anymore. We'll go up front and talk. Dad can catch our dinner."

SEA FLIGHT

Kevin shook his head. "Just don't ask me to eat fish tonight."

"No," Cassie said with a straight face. "We're having dinosaur stew."